Enjoy this book!

Please remember to return it on time
so that others may enjoy it too.

Manage your library account and
discover all we offer by visiting us
online at www.nashualibrary.org

Love your library? Tell a friend!

J

SPOTLIGHT ON EXPLORERS AND COLONIZATION™

GIOVANNI DA VERRAZZANO

Explorer of the Atlantic Coast of North America

MARTIN GITLIN

Rosen PUBLISHING®

New York

Published in 2017 by The Rosen Publishing Group, Inc.
29 East 21st Street, New York, NY 10010

First Edition

Library of Congress Cataloging-in-Publication Data

Names: Gitlin, Marty, author.
Title: Giovanni da Verrazzano : explorer of the Atlantic Coast of North
  America / Martin Gitlin.
Description: First edition. | New York : Rosen Publishing, 2017. | Series:
  Spotlight on explorers and colonization | Includes bibliographical
  references. | Audience: Grade 7 to 12.
Identifiers: LCCN 2016000176| ISBN 9781477788080 (library bound) | ISBN
  9781477788066 (pbk.) | ISBN 9781477788073 (6-pack)
Subjects: LCSH: Verrazzano, Giovanni da, 1485–1528. | America—Discovery and
  exploration—French. | Explorers—America—Biography. |
  Explorers—France—Biography.
Classification: LCC E133.V5 G57 2016 | DDC 910.92—dc23
LC record available at http://lccn.loc.gov/2016000176

Manufactured in the United States of America

CONTENTS

THE AGE OF EXPLORATION

Decades before Giovanni da Verrazzano embarked on his historic journey to what is now the United States, a race had begun. It was between the nations of Europe to find the best routes to Asia, where silk, spices, and other riches awaited them.

During the fifteenth century, Portuguese explorers sailed around Africa to find a new route. Next, explorers tried to reach Asia by sailing west across the Atlantic Ocean. In 1492 Christopher Columbus sailed across the Atlantic under the flag of Spain and landed in the West Indies. This inspired other explorers to set out for what would become known as the New World. England answered five years later when John Cabot

rediscovered what is now Canada.

Spain established its dominance of the exploration race with voyages to the Caribbean and beyond. Vasco Núñez de Balboa crossed Panama to discover the Pacific Ocean. Francisco Pizarro conquered the Inca Empire in Peru. Juan Ponce de León reached Florida in the mistaken notion he was on a Caribbean Island. But the figure after whom the newly discovered continents would be named was Amerigo Vespucci, an Italian explorer who sailed for Spain and Portugal.

AMERIGO INSPIRES "AMERICA"

Like Verrazzano, Amerigo Vespucci had Italian roots. Vespucci was born in Florence, Italy, and worked for the wealthy Medici family, who were very powerful there. In 1491, they sent him to manage their business in Spain. He became involved in the ship-outfitting business in the city of Seville, meeting Columbus around the time he made his first journey. A thirst for discovery soon motivated Vespucci to undertake journeys of his own.

Vespucci's most important journey took place in 1501 and 1502, when he explored the coast of South America for the king of Portugal. It was during this journey that he

AMERICUS VESPUCCI.

concluded that the lands he visited were not part of Asia but an entirely new continent. Columbus may have discovered the Americas, but it was Vespucci who recognized what he had found.

Vespucci wrote letters describing his voyage and arguing that the lands he explored were not part of Asia. Scholars across Europe, including a German mapmaker named Martin Waldseemüller, read these letters. In 1507, Waldseemüller made an updated map of the world showing a continent in the Atlantic Ocean, named "America" after the first name of the man who recognized it was a continent.

LIFE OF LUXURY

Giovanni da Verrazzano was born into a wealthy family. Members of his family held important jobs in the city government of Florence. The family's riches were evident by the countryside castle home in which they stayed during the summer to escape the city heat and avoid the dangers of contamination during the persistent plagues.

Giovanni was the third of four sons. The details of his birth are a bit unclear, but it seems most likely that he was born in 1485 in the town of Val di Greve, Italy. Little is known about his childhood and schooling, but his writings prove he received the finest education available and that he boasted a talent for mathematics and astronomy.

The city of Florence, Italy, spawned some of the most legendary explorers in world history, including Amerigo Vespucci and Giovanni da Verrazzano.

Young Giovanni also gained a love of literature from his father. He followed his dad into the raw wool and cloth industry. That took him to the town of Livorno, where as an older teenager he gained his first experiences with sailing. Meanwhile, his work in the business world would provide connections that would allow him to quench his thirst for exploration.

THE YOUNG TRAVELER

The French captain Thomas Aubert is not among the most famous of world travelers, but he played a major role in the budding career of Verrazzano as an explorer. Verrazzano was twenty-three when he accompanied Aubert on what was believed to have been a fishing expedition around Newfoundland, in what is now Canada, in 1508.

Aubert's crewmembers were actually not the first Europeans to sail to Newfoundland. The Viking explorer Leif Erikson had reached that island five centuries earlier. The Italian Giovanni Caboto, who sailed under the British flag and became known in

These are the shores of Newfoundland, which Verrazzano visited on his first trip to the New World, in 1508.

English as John Cabot, is also said to have visited Newfoundland.

Very little is known about Verrazzano's life after he returned from the journey with Aubert. Scholars think that he had most likely made France his home by this point in his life. However he does seem to have been in Lisbon, Portugal, in 1517, where a fateful meeting with one of the most legendary explorers in history may have helped inspire his next voyage to the New World.

INSPIRATION FROM OTHERS

The explorations of Amerigo Vespucci had long intrigued Verrazzano, but his meeting in Lisbon with the Portuguese explorer Ferdinand Magellan would prove especially significant for the Florentine navigator. At the time of the meeting, Magellan had yet to earn his special place in the history books as the leader of the first expedition to circumnavigate, or sail around, the globe. However he was already seeking backers for an expedition to find a route westward to the Indies, China, and the Moluccas (also known as the Spice Islands), all of which boasted spices much valued in Europe.

Verrazzano seems to have followed Magellan to Spain, where Magellan would eventually persuade the king to sponsor his trip around the world. However, Verrazzano did not end up accompanying Magellan on his voyage. For reasons still unknown, the two went their separate ways. At this point it seems that Verrazzano returned to France alongside his brother Girolamo. The two hoped to plan an excursion of their own.

CONVINCING
A KING

Hopeful European explorers of the sixteenth century needed two things before their dreams could become a reality: money and government permission.

Verrazzano was working on step one by 1522. He had been elected manager for the wealthy Rucellai family business. He was supervising the interests of powerful Florentine financiers and bankers. He had traveled to the cities of Paris and Lyon, where he worked with other merchants and businessmen. He lived in Dieppe, a port in France's Normandy region, which was an ideal place from which to organize an expedition.

The French king, Francis I, yearned to compete with Spain in the race to secure

Francis I, seen in a portrait painted in the 1520s by Jean Clouet, received thorough reports in a journal from Verrazzano about the historic exploration of much of the east coast of North America.

trade routes to Asia. He could not fund the voyage, for which Verrazzano requested four ships. The king offered only one, as well as five percent of the money needed to rig it. But those with whom Verrazzano worked had strong financial and political interests in finding trade routes to spice-rich Asia. They would not let him down. Verrazzano was ready to prepare for his historic journey.

GETTING HIS SHIPS IN SHAPE

Verrazzano was a man of many talents. He not only proved himself as a brilliant navigator and descriptive writer about his adventures, but also was a skilled businessman. He convinced merchants and bankers to fund his voyage by assuring them that the route he would take was shorter than those attempted by the Portuguese around Africa and south of Brazil.

The trip was soon financed by a group of private investors. The Verrazzano brothers worked tirelessly

throughout 1523 to prepare for their task. They supervised the preparation of the four ships that were to make the journey. They recruited fifty men for each vessel, including many scientists.

They gathered up enough supplies to last eight months. Included were arms and ammunition to fend off a possible attack by the Spanish. Verrazzano made certain that all would be well-fed, stocking up on bread, crackers, peas, beans, and herring, as well as freshly slaughtered cows and lambs.

Verrazzano made sure his ships had the navigational equimpent of the day, like the compass and traverse board in this illustration.

BON VOYAGE!

The start of the Verrazzano mission was not smooth sailing. The crew was forced to leave in mid-December 1523 to avoid conflict with Portugal, which feared the competition from France.

The four vessels were ready. Included was the flagship, which was baptized *Dauphine* in honor of the six-year-old heir to the French throne. It would lead the other three boats at all times. Verrazzano made certain he was in strict command.

Those three ships did not make the trip to the New World. A violent storm knocked two of them out of action and forced a stop in Brittany. Following repairs, the *Dauphine* and *Normanda* set sail again in January 1524, but the latter was soon disabled as

This portrait shows Francis III, the Duke of Brittany. As the oldest son of Francis I, the young Francis was the Dauphin, or heir to the crown of France. Verrazzano's ship, the *Dauphine*, was named in his honor.

well. The remaining crewmen assembled on the *Dauphine*.

A storm that Verrazzano said was as violent as any a navigator had ever endured slammed the ship on February 24. It tossed the *Dauphine* like a toy boat, but it and the men survived. The crew caught sight of what is now the United States in March. One incredible journey had ended. Another was about to begin.

BEFRIENDING THE NATIVES

Verrazzano described the first land he sighted—it was likely Cape Fear, North Carolina—as, "A new land, never before seen by ancient or modern eye." There would be more to see that no European had ever seen. Included were the Native Americans whose fires on the shore proved that the land was inhabited. At first, Verrazzano did not come ashore. After sailing briefly to the south, the *Dauphine* turned northward. Verrazzano knew that if he sailed south to Florida he risked confronting the Spaniards.

Verrazzano went ashore around the place he had first spotted land. A group of natives watched curiously before taking flight upon

This aerial view shows Cape Fear in North Carolina, where Verrazzano first sighted land on the North American continent.

the arrival of such odd-looking strangers. Eventually, some Native Americans returned. Verrazzano wrote that they showed "great joy" and were "astonished by our clothes, figures and whiteness."

Verrazzano was already expressing a respect for the Indian population that Columbus had not. In his trip to the Indies, Columbus wrote about their "ignorance" and claimed they would make good servants and slaves. Verrazzano wrote instead about the "prompt intellect" of the Indians he first encountered and would continue to praise other peoples he met during his journey.

Verrazzano was equally complimentary about the "beautiful plains and countryside" and "delighting aspect" of the multi-colored trees that "emit a sweet fragrance." But it was the Native Americans he met that appeared most noteworthy to him.

After Verrazzano's expedition moved northward along the coast, an event strengthened his respect for the native people. One of his crewmembers lost consciousness while trying to swim back to the boat after tossing knick-knacks to the natives on the shore. He lay half-dead on the beach.

The sailor eventually awoke and tried to escape the clutches of the natives, who attempted to calm him as they placed him on a sand dune and started a fire to warm him up. Verrazzano wrote about his appreciation for the natives, who then "with the greatest kindness… accompanied him to the sea,

This white-tailed deer is in the coastal forests of North Carolina. In his letter to the king of France, Verrazzano mentions the "abundance of animals, stags, deer, hares" that he saw in that area.

holding him close and embracing him" until the sailor had been returned to the ship. The friendships Verrazzano and his men would form with the Indian population had just begun.

ONWARD AND NORTHWARD

Though the crew might have yearned to enjoy the company of their native friends, their mission called them northward. They sailed along the Outer Banks, a chain of islands that extend from Cape Hatteras to what is now Virginia Beach. Verrazzano mistakenly thought that the Pacific Ocean—and the riches of China and India—lay on the other side of the islands. The waters he glimpsed on the other side of the islands were actually Pamlico, Albemarle, and Currituck Sounds, which separate the Outer Banks from mainland North America.

Verrazzano expressed wonder not just for the hunting skills and sturdy canoes of the Algonquian peoples he encountered in the

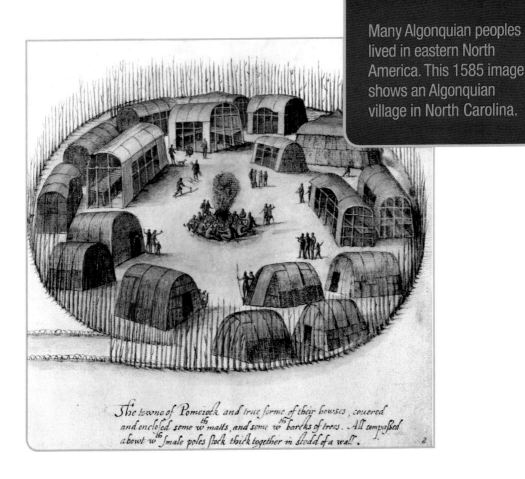

The towne of Pomeiock and true forme of their howses, couered and enclosed some wth matts, and some wth barcks of trees. All compassed abowt wth smale poles stuck thick together in stedd of a wall.

area, but also of the beauty and scent of the flowers and plants. Verrazzano wrote that he had reached "paradise on earth."

Soon it was time to move on. Verrazzano and his crew ventured north to what are today the Delaware and New Jersey coastlines, but found no place to anchor his ship. They continued sailing until they reached the body of water that is now known as New York Bay.

MANHATTAN TO RHODE ISLAND

A familiar sight met Verrazzano and his crew as they landed on Manhattan Island, a spot that is now the heart of New York City. It was a group of friendly and curious Native Americans. They rowed up and down the shore in their small boats to get a better glimpse of the strangers and the *Dauphine*, the biggest ship they had ever seen.

Verrazzano was particularly impressed with what he described as the "commodity and vastness" of the land, which boasted rich soil and impressive natural resources. He regretted it when bad weather forced his party to leave the area and continue northeast to what was likely Rhode Island, where they were greeted by Narragansett and Wampanoag tribespeople.

Giacomo Gastaldi's 1556 map draws on Verrazzano's account. "Port Réal" and "Port du Refuge" are Newport Bay and Narragansett Bay.

The sailors tossed them trinkets as a welcoming gesture. These were accepted joyfully, particularly the glass beads from Italy. The Native Americans were disinterested in the gold, iron, or steel deemed valuable by the Europeans. They also showed no curiosity about their weapons.

Verrazzano lauded his hosts as "sweet and gentle." He was particularly impressed with two Indians he believed to be kings who were "as beautiful of stature and build as I can possibly describe." He praised the

Native Americans as peaceful, friendly, and generous as they shared all they owned with him and his crew. They were so friendly, in fact, that Verrazzano granted his men fifteen days of rest and enjoyment at that very spot from April 21 to May 6.

Those two weeks provided Verrazzano time to explore. He discovered the land to be "so fertile that any kind of seed would produce excellent crop." Its staid beauty reminded him of the Florentine countryside.

Verrazzano was impressed by the circular homes made of bent saplings and woven straw mats in which the natives lived. He also wrote about how the Indians appeared free of disease, losing their lives only to old age. He was enamored with a culture that was so tied to nature, a concept foreign to Europeans. But he would soon discover to his dismay that not all Native Americans were so friendly.

HOSTILE HOSTS AND THE JOURNEY HOME

Cape Cod is now a popular vacation destination for millions of Americans. But Verrazzano bypassed it and sailed north to what is now the Maine coast, where he found thick forests of the kinds of trees that grow in colder climates, such as pines.

He also found the only unfriendly Indians his group would encounter. He wrote of the "crudity" of the "barbarous" Abenaki tribe, clad in skins of wolf and bear. Verrazzano quickly pegged them as hunters rather than natives skilled at farming. The only things they were interested in trading for were knives and fishing hooks. They behaved rudely to the strangers trying to communicate with them.

They even mocked the crew by bending over and flashing their bare butts at them.

A group of twenty-five well-armed crewmen disembarked, but were met with arrow fire from the howling natives. The expedition left what Verrazzano described as the "bad people" and traveled northward. They found land that was "more beautiful, without forests, with high mountains sloping toward the sea." By that time, however, their rations were running low. It was time to sail back to France.

PLANNING ANOTHER EXPEDITION

Upon Verrazzano's return to the city of Dieppe, the bells in every church rang out for hours, giving him and his crew a hero's welcome. Thousands of people gathered at the port to greet them. Verrazzano had drafted several copies of the report he had written for the king so friends and supporters could read all about the trip.

Verrazzano didn't believe that his return to France meant that his voyages were over. He announced to Francis I that the world was larger than previously thought. He had not proved whether the Americas were attached to Europe and Asia, so there was much more to explore.

Francis was agreeable to another journey, but an ongoing conflict with Charles V, the Holy Roman Emperor and king of Spain, was foremost on his mind. Soon the war was lost, and Francis was imprisoned by the Spanish. Verrazzano tried to get Henry VIII of England or John III of Portugal to back another voyage across the Atlantic, but was unsuccessful. His luck improved when Francis I was released in March 1526 after signing a treaty with Spain.

BOUND FOR BRAZIL

With the help of investors with whom Verrazzano had become quite familiar, the arrangements were eventually made for another voyage. The French admiral Philippe de Chabot also helped pave the way for the expedition. The three ships under Verrazzano's command set sail to Brazil in the spring of 1526.

There are conflicting stories about the route the ships took. Most agree that they crossed the Atlantic and sailed down the east coast of South America as far as the Amazon River. Some say they continued down the coast to the Straits of Magellan, although weather issues and mutinous crewmembers prevented all or some of the ships from passing through. Some accounts say the ships changed course and sailed toward the Cape of Good Hope, the southernmost point of Africa.

One thing we do know is that Verrazzano returned to France in 1527 with a load of Brazilwood. Brazilwood, from South America, is closely related to sappanwood, from Southeast Asia. A red dye, popular in Europe, could be made from both species. The Brazilwood satisfied the investors, but not Verrazzano. He still yearned to find a passage to the Indies.

VERRAZZANO'S FINAL VOYAGE

The details about the preparation for Verrazzano's final journey are lacking, but we do know that he sailed from Dieppe in the spring of 1528. It was a trip he would soon wish he had never made.

The expedition was once again headed for Brazil, but Verrazzano did not make it that far. After visiting several spots around the Caribbean, the expedition stopped at an island that is believed to have been Guadalupe. It was inhabited by cannibals, as Amerigo Vespucci had previously described. A group of six, including Verrazzano, disembarked to explore. The task did not appear dangerous as the beach was deserted.

Suddenly, however, a band of natives emerged from the forest, surrounded the men, and killed them. They ripped up Verrazzano's body and ate his flesh while his brother Girolamo watched from the boat in horror. Giorlamo and the other surviving members of the expedition eventually made their way back to France. In 1529 Girolamo made a map of the word that reflected what he had learned on his voyages with his brother. It was a big improvement on earlier maps of the New World.

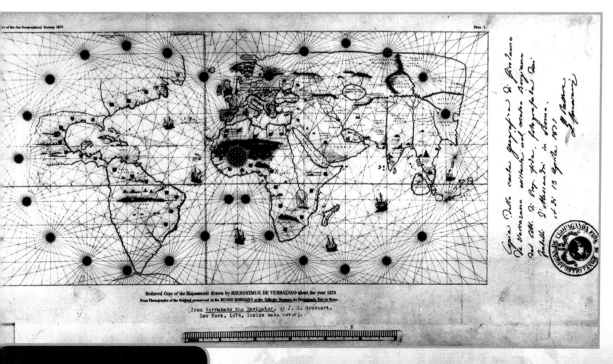

Girolamo de Verrazzano's 1529 Map.

THE LEGACY OF GIOVANNI DA VERRAZZANO

Verrazzano was not merely an ambitious world traveler. He was one of the most important figures in the European exploration of the New World. Verrazzano was the first to provide proof of the North American continent. Through his keen calculations, he even gave an indication of its size. He recognized the economic potential of the land, commenting on which places had dense forests or fertile fields. While he may have been wrong about some of the geographical details—such as thinking Pamlico Sound was an ocean—he got plenty of others right.

Gloria italiana rivendicata in America: inaugurazione del monumento a G. da Verrazzano che primo scoprì la baia di New York.

(Disegno di A. Beltrame)

The intelligence, observational skills, and writing talent of Verrazzano were evident throughout his venture, which he chronicled meticulously. His letter to Francis I describing his 1524 voyage is far more descriptive than the records that have survived from other European explorers of the same period. The letter is an invaluable source of information about eastern North America and its inhabitants before both were changed by contact with Europeans.

Verrazzano demonstrated a depth and insight that many other explorers lacked. He had an open mind in regard to the Native Americans that he and his crew encountered on every stop of his journey. He preferred friendship to mistrust.

While other explorers such as Columbus viewed the natives as potential slave labor, he wrote gushingly about their culture and their friendliness. He was curious about their lives and aware that language difficulties limited his understanding of their culture.

None of his voyages would have been possible had Verrazzano not been a skilled businessman as well. His ability to convince merchants, bankers, and other people of influence in Florence and throughout France of the economic benefits of his voyages allowed him to make discoveries that would change the world.

It is no wonder that modern-day America has honored him. For this one must look no further than the suspension bridge that connects the New York City boroughs of Staten Island and Brooklyn. It is called the Verrazano-Narrows Bridge.

GLOSSARY

ammunition Material fired from a weapon.

barbarous Wild and savage.

cannibals People who eat other people, either for food or as part of a ritual.

chronicled Detailed an experience through writing.

circumnavigate To sail around something.

contamination Getting sick through contact with something bad or unclean.

disembarked Left a vehicle, in particular a ship.

expedition A trip or voyage with a particular goal.

fertile Good for growing crops.

financiers People who provide money needed for a business venture.

flagship The lead ship in a voyage.

intellect A person's mental capability.

investors People who spend money in seeking future financial benefits.

merchants People who make money by buying and selling goods or raw materials.

mutinous Rebelling against the people in charge, particularly on a ship or in the military.

navigator Someone who explores by sea.

outfitting Getting together the goods or equipment needed for a task.

plagues Outbreaks of disease that kill many people.

saplings Small trees or tree trunks.

The Gilder Lehrman Institute of American History
49 West 45th Street, 6th Floor
New York, NY 10036
(646) 366-9666
Website: http://www.gilderlehrmen.org
This nonprofit organization is dedicated to improving
history education through programs for schools,
teachers, and students. The group's website also
provides access to more than 60,000 historical
documents, including writings from the age of
exploration.

The Mariners' Museum and Park
100 Museum Drive
Newport News, VA 23606
(757) 596-2222
Website: http://www.marinersmuseum.org/
This group of museums holds some of the largest
collections of artifacts and historical objects on
the exploration of the Western Hemisphere. The
museum also maintains a website with information
about history's greatest explorers.

National Center for History in the Schools
6265 Bunche Hall
Box 951473
Los Angeles, CA 90095

(310) 825-4702

Website: http://www.nchs.ucla.edu/world-history-for
-us-all

This organization helps students understand the past
by linking specific subject matter to larger historical
patterns.

Organization of American Historians
112 North Bryan Avenue
Bloomington, IN 47408
(812) 855-7311

Website: http://www.oah.org/

The mission of this organization is to promote
excellence in the research and teaching of American
history. Members include a mix of professors,
teachers, museum curators, students, and more.

Websites

Because of the changing nature of Internet links,
Rosen Publishing has developed an online list of
websites related to the subject of this book. This site is
updated regularly. Please use this link to access the list:

http://www.rosenlinks.com/SEC/verra

Bakeless, John. *America as Seen by Its First Explorers: The Eyes of Discovery*. Mineola, NY: Dover Publications, 2011.

Dalkeith, Lena. *Stories from French History*. Laguna Beach, CA: Quintessential Classics, 2015.

Faust, Daniel R. *New York's European Explorers*. New York: PowerKids Press, 2014.

Fraser, Ian D. *Amerigo Vespucci for Kids!: The Amazing Explorer Who Discovered the Truth About the New World*. Amazon Digital Services, 2015.

Gimpel, Diane Marczely. *A Timeline History of Early American Indian Peoples*. Minneapolis, MN: 21st Century Publishing, 2014.

History Year by Year. New York: DK Publishing, 2013.

Kramme, Michael. *Exploring North America*. Quincy, IL: Mark Twain Media, 2012.

Pletcher, Kenneth. *The Age of Exploration: From Christopher Columbus to Ferdinand Magellan*. New York: Rosen Publishing, 2013.

Ross, Stewart. *Into the Unknown: How Great Explorers Found Their Way by Land, Sea, and Air*. Sommerville, MA: Candlewick Press, 2014.

Verrazzano, Giovanni da. *Verrazzano's Voyage Along the Atlantic Coast of North America*. Providence, RI: Scholar's Choice, 2015.

BIBLIOGRAPHY

Dunlap, Thomas R. *On the Edge: Mapping North America's Coasts.* New York, NY: Oxford University Press, 2012.

Heritage: Newfoundland and Labrador. "John Cabot's Voyage of 1497." Retrieved December 18, 2015 (http://www.heritage.nf.ca).

Heritage: Newfoundland and Labrador. "The International Fishery of the 16th Century." Retrieved December 18, 2015 (http://www.heritage.nf.ca).

Hoffman, Paul E. *A New Andalucia and a Way to the Orient: The American Southeast During the Sixteenth Century.* Baton Rouge, LA: Louisiana State University Press, 2015.

"Giovanni da Verrazzano." Mariners' Museum: Age of Exploration. Retrieved December 19, 2015 (http://exploration.marinersmuseum.org).

"Giovanni da Verrazzano: Letter to King Francis I of 8 July 1524." National Humanities Center. Retrieved December 20, 2015 (http://nationalhumanitiescenter.org).

Masini, Giancarlo. *How Florence Invented America.* New York, NY: Marsilio Publishers, 1998.

Schwartz, Seymour I. *The Mismapping of America.* Rochester, NY: University of Rochester Press, 2008.

INDEX

About the Author

Martin Gitlin has had over 100 books published since 2006, including dozens in the realms of history and social studies. During his eleven years as a journalist, he won more than 45 awards, including first place for general excellence from *The Associated Press* in 1996. That organization also selected him as one of the top four feature writers in the state of Ohio in 2002. Gitlin lives in Cleveland, Ohio, with his wife and three kids.

Photo Credits

Designer: Nicole Russo; Editor: Amelie von Zumbusch; Photo Researcher: Sherri Jackson